DRIVING SKILLS

YOUR DRIVING TEST

London: HMSO

Developed and prepared by COMIND

Design and writing:
Nick Lynch

Illustrations:
Vicky Squires

© Copyright Controller HMSO 1990
First published 1990

ISBN 0 11 550976 3

"Safe Driving for Life"

This book is aimed at those who are currently learning to drive a car or ride a motorcycle or who are about to learn to drive or ride. There are many myths about driving, riding motorcycles and even more about the driving test. We hope to dispel these by giving you sound advice on what you need to learn and how driving tests are conducted.

The Driving Standards Agency (DSA) is an Agency of the Department of Transport. It is responsible for all driving tests, the Register of Approved Driving Instructors, and is the authoritative body for matters relating to driving and riding techniques.

Each year nearly one million people decide they want to learn either to drive a car or to ride a motorcycle. You and most of the others will go on to take a driving test.

The purpose of the driving test is to see if you can drive your vehicle safely on the road. Equally important is to develop the right attitude towards driving, and to drive at all times with responsibility, and with consideration for those who are sharing the road with you. Only those who can do this earn the right to drive a vehicle without supervision, without L-plates, and on motorways.

The test is just one stage in your driving or riding career. You should not assume that if you pass the test, you are a good driver or rider with nothing more to learn. The instruction you have before the test is the foundation for gaining knowledge, skills and experience.

Your driving career started the moment you decided that you wanted to be able to drive a car or ride a motorcycle on the road. The fact that you are now reading this book confirms that your aim is *safe driving for life.*

Keith Cameron
Chief Driving Examiner
Driving Standards Agency

Contents

Section 1 — Before the Test

How to use this book 1
The driving test 2
Preparing for your driving test 4
When you are ready for the test 6
How to apply for the test 7
Before attending for the test 8

Section 2 — The Driving Test

The eyesight test 9
Knowledge you must show 10
Before you start the engine 11
The car controls 12
The other controls 15
Using the main car controls — moving off 16
The emergency stop 17
Reversing round a corner 18
Reverse parking 19
Turning in the road 20
Using the mirrors 21
Giving signals 22
Acting on signs and signals 23
Controlling your speed 24
Making progress 25
Hazards: The correct routine 26
Road junctions, including roundabouts 27
Overtaking 29
Meeting other vehicles and passing stationary vehicles 30
Crossing the path of other vehicles 31
Pedestrian crossings 32
Selecting a safe place to stop 34
Awareness and anticipation 35

Continued ☛

Contents (cont'd)

Section 3 — The Motorcycle Test
Preparation and training   36
Compulsory training for motorcycle learners   37

    Element 1: Introduction   37
    Element 2: Practical on-site training   38
    Element 3: Practical on-site riding   39
    Element 4: Practical on-road training   40
    Element 5: Practical on-road riding   41

    The motorcycle test   42
    Special features   42

Section 4 — Recommended syllabus for learning to drive   43

Section 5 — Additional information   46

Section 6 — List of DSA offices and other useful addresses   48

This book will help you to

- Learn to drive competently
- Prepare for and pass your driving test

Section 2 gives the test requirements and sound advice, simply and clearly.

Consult it regularly while you are learning and use it to check your progress.

Section 4 gives the Driving Test Syllabus which lists the precise requirements. Refer to it when you need precise information on a particular aspect of the test.

If you are a learner motorcyclist, Section 3 will tell you all you need to know about compulsory basic training.

This book is one of the three important factors in your training: the other two are

- A good instructor (see page 4)
- Your attitude

You must manage your own learning.

Aim to be a competent and safe driver or motorcyclist, and not just to pass the test.

Driving is a life skill.

Your driving test is only the first step.

Further essential reading for all drivers

The Driving Standards Agency's manual *Driving* (HMSO) sets out sound, safe and well-tried driving methods.

It's the Approved Driving Instructor's 'Bible'.

You can buy it from any good bookshop.

The Driving Test

The driving test is straightforward

You will pass if

you can satisfy the examiner that you can

- Drive safely
- Do the set exercises
- Show enough knowledge of the Highway Code

Does the standard of the test vary?

No! All examiners are trained to carry out tests to the same standard.

Test routes

- Are as uniform as possible
- Include a range of typical road and traffic conditions

You should have the same result from different examiners or at different Driving Test Centres.

Are examiners supervised?

Yes! They are closely supervised. A senior officer may sit in on your test.

Don't worry about this.

The senior officer won't be examining you, but making sure the examiner is testing you properly.

Since the senior officer will not interfere with the test or the result, just carry on as if he or she wasn't there.

What will the examiner want from me?

The examiner will want to see you drive safely and competently under various road and traffic conditions.

He (or she) will

- Give you directions clearly and in good time
- Ask you to carry out set exercises

The examiner will be understanding and sympathetic, and will make every effort to put you at ease.

However, to avoid distracting you, the examiner will say as little as possible while you're driving.

How should I drive during the test?

Drive in the way your instructor has taught you.

If you make a mistake, don't worry. It might be minor and may not affect your result.

The examiner will be looking for an overall safe standard and is unlikely to fail you for just one minor mistake.

How long will the test last?

About 35 minutes.

 What will the test include?

Apart from general driving which we will talk about later, your test will include

- An eyesight test
- Special exercises, such as
  - an emergency stop
  - reversing round a corner
  - turning in the road
  - reverse parking
- Questions on
  - the Highway Code
  - other motoring matters

 What's the order of the test?

The eyesight test is first.

If you fail that, the test will not go ahead.

After the eyesight test, the order is up to the examiner.

 What about the special exercises?

The first special exercise, usually the emergency stop, normally comes after a short drive.

The examiner will be as helpful as possible, and will

- Ask you to pull up at the left side of the road
- Explain any one of the special exercises and ask you to carry it out

Make sure you understand!

If you're not sure about anything, ask! The examiner will explain again.

The other special exercises will be spread over the test route.

 What's the purpose of the test?

The driving test is designed to see if

- You can drive safely
- You know and understand the Highway Code
- You understand other motoring matters, such as
  - what causes skids and how to control them
  - the importance of car maintenance

The test ensures that all drivers reach a minimum standard.

When you have passed

You'll be allowed to drive

- Without L-plates
- Unsupervised
- On motorways

However, it takes lots of practice to become a really skilled driver. Further tuition is recommended.

Preparing for your driving test

Your Provisional Driving Licence

You must hold a Provisional Driving Licence before you take any instruction on the road.

Ask for the application form at your local Post Office.

Why you should use an Approved Driving Instructor (ADI)

An Approved Driving Instructor is approved by the Driving Standards Agency to teach learner drivers for payment.

The Driving Standards Agency is responsible for maintaining and checking the standards for all ADIs.

You must use an ADI

If you want to learn to drive and you want to pay someone to teach you.

It is unlikely that anyone except an ADI will have the experience, knowledge and training to teach you properly.

ADIs must

- Pass a difficult examination
- Reach and keep up a high standard of instruction
- Be registered with the Driving Standards Agency
- Display an ADI identification certificate on the windscreen of the tuition vehicle

Friends and relatives

If you are taking lessons with an ADI, it's a good idea to take extra practice with a friend or relative.

Ask your ADI for advice on this.

Take advice from your ADI on

- All aspects of driving
- What books to read
- When you will be ready for the test
- How to practise

How to choose an ADI

- Ask friends and relatives
- Choose an instructor
  - who has a good reputation
  - is reliable and punctual
  - whose car suits you

178611

Department of
Transport
Approved Driving
Instructor

When you practise ...

You must have with you a person who

- Has held a full UK licence for at least three years
- Is at least 21 years of age

Vehicle insurance

The vehicle you practise in must be properly insured for you to drive. If it's not, you'll be

- Driving an uninsured vehicle
- Committing a traffic offence

Don't risk it!

How and where to practise

Practise

- On as many different types of road as you can
- In all sorts of traffic conditions — even in the dark

Practise

- The exercises included in the test, but don't concentrate solely on them

Practise

- On dual carriageways where the upper speed limit applies

You may be asked to drive on such roads during the test.

What to avoid when you practise

- Never block traffic

Drivers are very tolerant of learners, but don't try their patience too much

- Never annoy local residents

For example, by practising emergency stops in quiet, residential streets

- Never practise on test routes

The Highway Code

You must

- Know and understand the Highway Code
- Obey it during the test
- Answer questions on it

So study it carefully!

The Highway Code

HMSO

The Department of Transport

When you are ready for the test

 When will I be ready for the test?

When you can show that you have reached the standard set in this book. Not before.

The learners who pass first time are the ones who are well instructed and get in plenty of practice.

They pass because **they wait until they're ready.**

 How will I know when I'm ready?

Your ADI will tell you. He (or she) has the knowledge and experience.

You must be able to drive

- *Consistently* well and with confidence
- Without assistance and guidance from your instructor

If you can't, you aren't ready for the test.

Most people who fail do so because they haven't had enough instruction and practice.

They waste their money and the examiner's time.

The application form

- Ask for form DL26 at any Post Office or Driving Standards Agency Regional Office. You'll find the address in Section 6.

If you wish to take the test in the Welsh language, please indicate this on the form.

- Complete the form, and send it with the appropriate fee to your Driving Standards Agency Regional Office
- Apply well before the time you want to be tested
- Give the earliest date you think you'll be ready

Special circumstances

To make sure that enough time is allowed for your test, it would help the DSA to know

- If you are profoundly deaf
- If you are restricted in any way in your movements
- If you have any disability which may affect your driving

So, if any of these applies to you, please write this on your application form.

If you can't speak English or are deaf, you are allowed to bring an interpreter.

Your test appointment

Your DSA Regional Office will send you an appointment card.

This will give you

- The time and date of your appointment
- The address of the Driving Test Centre
- Other important information

Postponing your test appointment

Contact your DSA Regional Office where you booked your test if

- The date or time on the card is not suitable
- You want to postpone or cancel the test

You must give at least 10 clear working days notice, (that is, two weeks—longer if there is a bank holiday) not counting

- The day the Office received your request
- The day of the test

If you don't give enough notice, you will lose your fee.

Before attending for the test

Your driving licence

Make sure that you have your provisional driving licence with you, and that you have signed it.

If you don't, you'll need some other form of identity. The following are acceptable

- Any driving licence issued in
  - Great Britain, Northern Ireland, the Channel Islands, or the Isle of Man
  - an EC member state
  - a country whose driving licences can be exchanged for a United Kingdom Driving Licence
- A passport
- An International Driving Permit
- A British Forces Licence
- An identity card issued by your employer. This must show
  - your name written in roman letters (such as ordinary printing)
  - your photograph
  - your signature

Remember, it's up to you to satisfy the examiner. Otherwise, your test will be cancelled.

Your test vehicle

Make sure that the vehicle you intend to drive during your test is

- Legally roadworthy and has a current test certificate, if it is over the prescribed age
- Fully covered by insurance for its present use and for you to drive
- Properly licensed with the correct disc displayed on the windscreen
- Displaying L-plates where required, which are visible from the front and rear

If you overlook any of these

- Your test may be cancelled
- You could lose your fee

What the test requires

You must satisfy the examiner that, in good daylight, you can read a vehicle number-plate with letters 79.4mm (3.1 inches) high.

Minimum distance

- 20.5 metres (about 67 feet), or
- 12.2 metres (about 40 feet) if you are operating a pedestrian-controlled vehicle.

If you need glasses

or contact lenses, wear them.

Continue to wear them during the test and whenever you drive or ride.

How the examiner will test you

Before you get into your car, the examiner will point to a vehicle and ask you to read the number-plate.

If you are unable to read the number-plate, the examiner will measure the exact distance and repeat the test.

If you fail the eyesight test

If you can't satisfy the examiner that your eyesight is up to the standard required

- You will have failed your driving test
- Your test will go no further

If you normally wear glasses or contact lenses, wear them always when you drive or ride.

Knowledge you must show

The Highway Code

You must

- Show knowledge of the Highway Code
- Obey the rules set out in it

Other motoring matters

You must also show knowledge of other motoring matters, including

- Matters not covered in the Highway Code, such as
  - tyre wear
  - car and road safety
  - basic car maintenance
- Behaviour and road holding of vehicles in bad weather

You must show that you know the Highway Code and that you can apply it.

How the examiner will test you

At the end of the test, your examiner will ask you some questions on the Highway Code and on other motoring matters.

You must answer these to the examiner's satisfaction, although small errors may not cause you to fail.

You will also be asked to identify some traffic signs.

But remember!

Knowing is not enough.

You must demonstrate your knowledge as you drive.

What the examiner wants to see

Before you start your engine, you must always check that

1. Your seat is correctly adjusted and comfortable

2. Your driving mirrors are correctly adjusted

3. Your seat belt is correctly adjusted and comfortable

4. The handbrake is on

5. The gear lever is in neutral

So develop good habits and practise while you're learning.

X **Faults you must avoid**

When the car is moving, never

- Adjust your seat. This is extremely dangerous
- Adjust your seat belt
- Adjust any of your driving mirrors
- Hold on to the handbrake or gear lever unnecessarily

The car controls

 What the test requires

You must satisfy your examiner that you understand the functions of all the controls and can use them

- Smoothly
- Correctly
- Safely
- At the right time

The main controls are

- Accelerator
- Clutch
- Footbrake
- Handbrake
- Steering
- Gears

You must

- Understand what these controls do
- Be able to use them competently

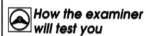 **How the examiner will test you**

For this aspect of driving, there is no special exercise.

The examiner will watch you carefully to see how you use these controls.

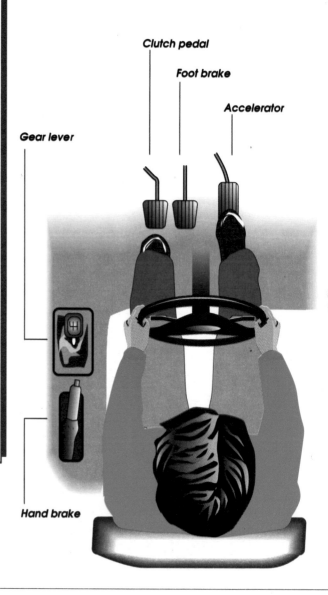

Clutch pedal

Foot brake

Accelerator

Gear lever

Hand brake

✔ Skills you must master

Accelerator and clutch

- Balance accelerator and clutch to pull away smoothly
- Accelerate evenly to gain speed
- When stopping the car, press the clutch in just before the car stops

Gears

- Choose the right gear for your speed and the road conditions
- Change gear in good time before a hazard or junction

Footbrake

- Brake in good time
- Brake lightly in most situations

Handbrake

- Know how and when to apply the handbrake

✗ Faults you must avoid

Accelerator

- Accelerating fiercely, especially making the tyres screech — distracting or alarming other road users

Clutch

- Jerky and uncontrolled use of the clutch when moving off or changing gear

Gears

- Taking your eyes off the road when you change gear
- Coasting with
  - clutch pedal pressed in, or
  - gear lever in neutral
- Holding on to the gear lever unnecessarily

Footbrake

- Avoid braking harshly, except in emergency

Handbrake

- Never apply the handbrake before the car has stopped
- Never move off with the handbrake on

Typical gearbox layouts

The car controls — steering

Steering

- Keep a steady course
- Place your hands on the steering wheel in either the 'ten-to-two' or 'quarter-to-three' positions
- When turning a corner, begin turning the steering wheel at the right time

Steering

- Never turn too early when steering around a corner. If you do, you risk
  - cutting the corner when turning right and putting other road users at risk
  - striking the kerb when turning left
- Never turn too late. You could put other road users at risk by
  - swinging wide at left turns
  - overshooting right turns
- Avoid crossing your hands on the steering wheel
- Never allow the wheel to spin back after turning

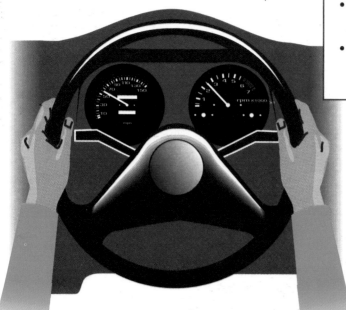

Correct hand positions for steering

The other controls

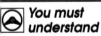

You must understand

- The functions of *all* controls and switches which have a bearing on road safety

For example:
- indicators
- lights
- windscreen wipers
- demisters

- The meaning of gauges or other displays on the instrument panel

For example:
- speedometer
- various warning lights

Safety checks

You should also be able to

- Carry out routine safety checks that do not require tools

- Identify defects especially with
    - steering
    - brakes
    - tyres
    - seat belts
    - lights
    - reflectors
    - horn
    - rear view mirrors
    - speedometer
    - exhaust system
    - direction indicators
    - windscreen wipers and washers

- Describe the safety factors relating to vehicle loading.

Note: This is expected to become a requirement of the test.

Using the main car controls — moving off

 What the test requires

You must satisfy the examiner that you can move off

- Safely
- Under control
1. On the flat
2. From behind a parked car
3. On a hill, if practicable

 How the examiner will test you

The examiner will watch your use of the controls each time you move off.

 Skills you must show

1. Use your mirrors. Signal if necessary
2. Before you move off, look around for
   - Traffic
   - Pedestrians outside the range of your mirrors
3. Move off under control making balanced and safe use of
   - Accelerator
   - Clutch
   - Brakes
   - Steering
4. Use the correct gear

 Faults you must avoid

- Pulling out without looking
- Causing other road users to stop or alter their course
- Accelerating wildly, especially making your tyres screech — distracting or alarming other road users
- Moving off in too high a gear
- Failing to judge the 'biting' point of the clutch, and stalling the engine .

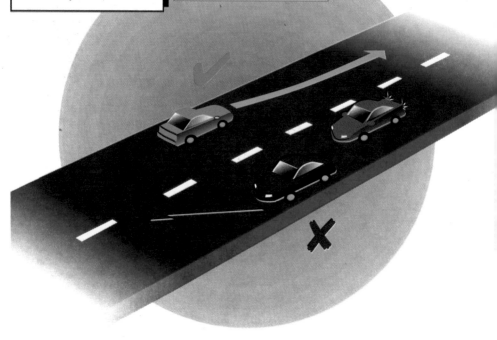

What the test requires

In an emergency you must be able to stop the car

- As quickly as possible
- Safely under control
- Without locking the wheels

 Skills you must show

Stopping the car

- In the shortest safe distance
- Under full control
- Without risk to other road users

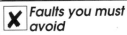 **Faults you must avoid**

- Skidding out of control
- Allowing the car to swing off course

 How the examiner will test you

The examiner will

1. Ask you to pull up at the side of the road
2. Ask you to make an emergency stop when you are given a signal
3. Demonstrate the signal to you

When the examiner gives the signal, try to stop the car as you would in a real emergency.

- You must react quickly
- Try to stop in a straight line
- Take special care if the road is wet

If you have to make a real emergency stop during the test, the examiner might not ask you to do this exercise.

Reversing round a corner

 What the test requires

You must satisfy your examiner that you can reverse your car

- Smoothly
- Correctly
- Safely
- Under full control

 Skills you must master

- Reversing under full control
- Keeping reasonably close to the kerb, without striking or mounting it

 Faults you must avoid

- Mounting the kerb
- Swinging out wide
- Keeping too far from the kerb
- Causing danger to other road users

 How the examiner will test you

The examiner will
- Ask you to pull up just before a side road on the left
- Point out the side road and ask you to reverse into it

When your examiner asks you
1. Make sure you can carry out the exercise correctly and safely
2. Check traffic and road conditions in all directions
3. Reverse around the corner, keeping a good lookout for traffic or pedestrians
4. Straighten up your car and continue to reverse for a reasonable distance
5. Pull up in a safe position and wait for your examiner's next instruction

Your seat belt

You may undo your seat belt for the whole exercise.

Do so only if it interferes with your driving, and don't forget to re-fasten it before you move forward after the exercise.

Note: If your car has no clear view to the rear, your examiner may ask you to reverse into a turning on the right.

Remember!

Your car will swing out at the front as you reverse around the corner, so keep a good lookout for other road users.

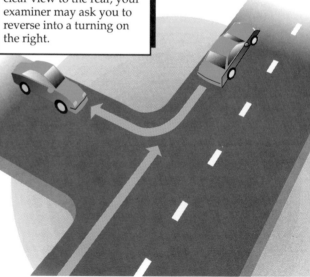

Reverse parking exercise

Note: To be added to the test requirements on April 1st, 1991. From that date you might be asked to do this exercise instead of turning in the road or reversing round a corner.

 What the test requires

You must be able to park your car safely at the kerb by reversing into the space of about two car lengths.

 How the examiner will test you

When your examiner points out a parked car and asks you to reverse park behind it

1. Drive alongside the parked car and position your car so that you can carry out the exercise correctly and safely

2. Reverse into the space behind the parked car, within the space of about two car lengths

3. Stop reasonably close to the kerb

 Skills you must master

Safe, steady and controlled parking

 Faults you must avoid

- Getting too close to the parked car
- Mounting the kerb
- Swinging your car from side to side
- Parking too far from the kerb
- Causing danger to other road users

Remember!

Keep a good lookout for traffic and pedestrians all the time.

Turning in the road

 What the test requires

You must be able to turn your car around in the road

- So it faces in the opposite direction
- Using forward and reverse gears

This will take you at least three moves, but make as few as you can.

 How the examiner will test you

Your examiner will

- Indicate a suitable place and ask you to pull up
- Ask you to turn around in the road.

1. Before you begin, be sure you can carry out the exercise correctly and safely. As driver, you are responsible

2. Make sure the road is clear in both directions.

3. Drive forward in first gear and turn your car to your right with the steering wheel turned to the right as much as possible

4. Steer briskly to the left just before you pull up close to the opposite kerb

5. Make sure the road is clear in both directions

6. Reverse, turning your steering wheel to the left as much as possible

7. Steer briskly to the right just before you pull up close to the kerb behind you

8. Repeat steps 3 to 7 until your car is facing the opposite direction

 Skills you must master

You must

- Control your car smoothly
- Make proper use of the
  - accelerator
  - clutch
  - brakes
  - steering
- Show awareness of other road users. Keep a good lookout!

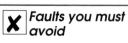 **Faults you must avoid**

- Mounting the kerb. (Try not to touch it)
- Causing danger to other road users

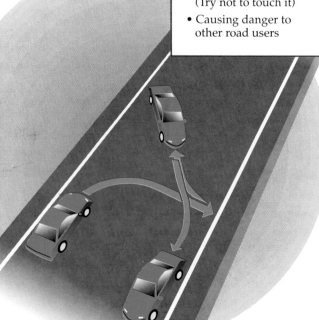

What the test requires

Make sure you use your mirrors effectively

- Before any manoeuvre
- To keep up to date on what is happening behind you

Check carefully before

- Moving off
- Signalling
- Changing direction
- Turning left or right
- Overtaking or changing lane
- Slowing down or stopping
- Opening your car door

 How the examiner will test you

For this aspect of driving, there is no special test.

The examiner will watch your use of mirrors as you drive.

 Skills you must show

- Using the Mirror-Signal-Manoeuvre (MSM) routine. Practise
  - looking before you signal
  - looking and signalling before you act
- Acting sensibly and safely on what you see in the mirrors
- Being aware that the mirrors will not show everything behind you

 Faults you must avoid

- Manoeuvring without looking in the mirror
- Not acting on what you see when you look in the mirror

Just looking is not enough!

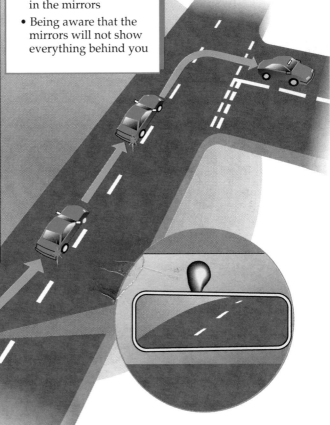

Giving signals

What the test requires

You must signal

- To let others know what you intend to do
- To help other road users, including pedestrians
- In plenty of time

You must only use the signals shown in the Highway Code.

Your signals must help other road users

- To understand what you intend to do
- To react safely

Always make sure your signal is cancelled after use.

How the examiner will test you

For this aspect of driving, there is no special exercise.

The examiner will watch carefully how you use your signals as you drive.

Skills you must master

Giving signals

- Clearly
- In good time
- Using mechanical aids such as indicators

You should also know and be able to give arm signals when necessary.

Faults you must avoid

- Giving signals carelessly
- Misleading other road users
- Waving at pedestrians to cross the road

What the test requires

You must

- Be able to understand
  - all traffic signs
  - road markings
- React to them safely and in good time

At the beginning of the test, the examiner will ask you to follow the road ahead.

Do so unless traffic signs tell you otherwise.

 Traffic lights

You must

- Act correctly at traffic lights
- When the green light shows, check that the road is clear before proceeding

Signals by officers

You must obey the signals given by

- police officers
- traffic wardens
- school crossing patrols

GIVE WAY
50 yds

30

Controlling your speed

 What the test requires

You must make good progress along the road, bearing in mind

- Road conditions
- Traffic
- Weather
- Road signs and speed limits

 How the examiner will test you

For this aspect of driving, there is no special exercise.

The examiner will watch carefully your control of speed as you drive.

 Skills you must master

You must

- Take great care in the use of speed
- Make sure you can stop safely, well within the distance you can see to be clear
- Leave a safe distance between yourself and other vehicles
- Leave extra distance on wet or slippery roads
- Drive at a steady speed within the speed limit

 Faults you must avoid

- Driving too fast for the road or traffic conditions
- Changing your speed erratically

Select a speed to suit road and traffic conditions

Making progress

⬛ What the test requires

You must

- Make progress along the road
- Drive at a speed appropriate to road and traffic conditions
- Move off at junctions as soon as it is safe to do so

⬛ How the examiner will test you

For this aspect of driving, there is no special exercise.

The examiner will watch your driving, and will want to see you

- Making reasonable progress along the road
- Keeping up with traffic
- Showing confidence and sound judgement

Avoid waiting when it is safe to proceed

✔ Skills you must master

You must be able to

- Choose the correct speed for
  - the type of road
  - the type and density of traffic
  - the weather and visibility
- Approach all hazards at a safe speed without
  - being too cautious
  - interfering with the progress of other traffic

✖ Faults you must avoid

You must not

- Drive too slowly. You could hold up traffic
- Be overcautious and stop or wait when it's safe and normal to proceed

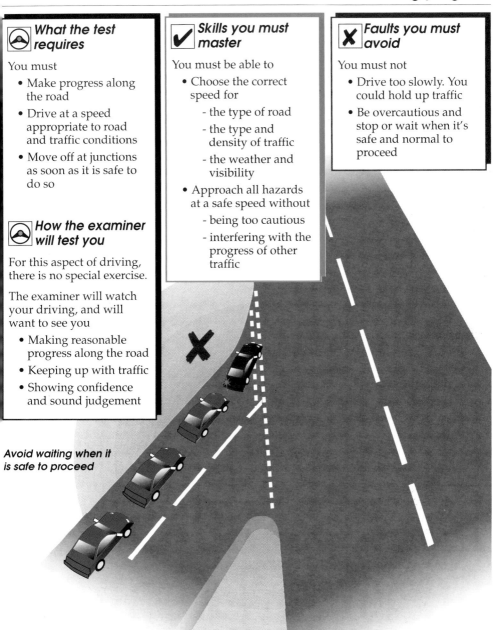

What is a hazard?

Hazards involve you in some kind of danger to yourself or others.

To identify hazards, look well ahead for

- Road junctions and roundabouts
- Parked vehicles
- Cyclists
- Pedestrian crossings

If you can identify the hazard and know the effect it might have, you can take the right action.

That action varies with the type of hazard.

 What the test requires

Approaching a hazard

Mirror-Signal-Manoeuvre (MSM routine)

Always use this routine when approaching a hazard.

M - Mirror

Check the position of traffic behind you.

S - Signal

Signal your intention to change course or slow down. Signal in good time.

M - Manoeuvre

A manoeuvre is any change of speed or position, from slowing or stopping the car to turning off a busy main road.

What the test requires

You should

• Use the MSM routine when you approach a junction or roundabout

• Position your car correctly. Adjust your speed. Stop if necessary

• If the road has lane markings, use the correct lane. In a one-way street, choose that lane as soon as you can

• If the road has no lane markings

   - when turning left, keep to the left, and watch out for

     motorcyclists and cyclists coming up on your left

     pedestrians crossing

   - when turning right, keep as close to the centre of the road as is safe

• Make sure you take effective observation before you enter a junction

 How the examiner will test you

For this aspect of driving, there is no special exercise.

The examiner will watch carefully and take account of your

• Use of the MSM routine

• Position and speed of approach

• Observation and judgement

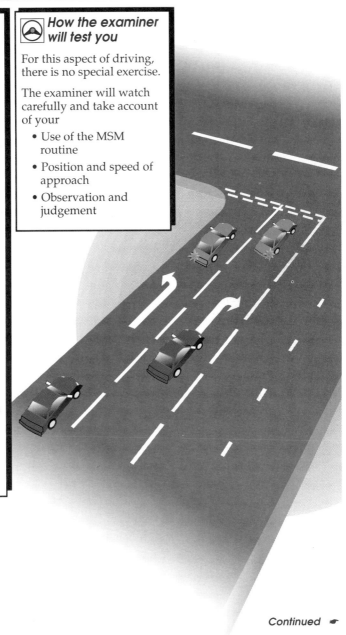

Continued ☛

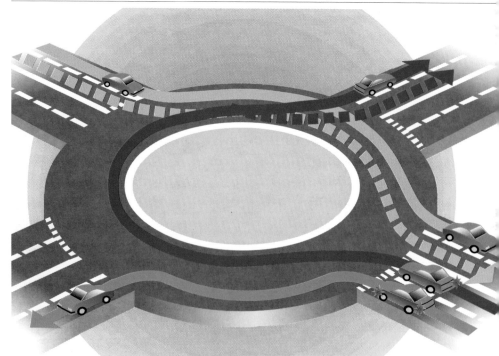

✔ Skills you must master

You must be able to

- Read the road signs and markings accurately (stop signs, give way signs, and so on)
- Judge the correct approach speed
- Slow down in good time and without braking hard
- Judge the speed of traffic, especially at roundabouts and when joining major roads

✘ Faults you must avoid

- Approaching the junction at the wrong speed
- Positioning and turning incorrectly
- Stopping or waiting unnecessarily
- Entering a junction unsafely

What the test requires

When overtaking you must

- Allow enough room
- Give motorcyclists and cyclists at least as much room as a car. They can swerve or wobble suddenly
- Allow enough space after overtaking. Don't cut in

Do not overtake if the road is too narrow or your view too limited.

How the examiner will test you

For this aspect of driving, there is no special exercise.

The examiner will watch carefully and take account of your

- Use of the MSM routine
- Reactions to road and traffic conditions
- Handling of the controls

Skills you must master

You must be able to

- Take stock of the speed and positions of all traffic, such as
  - traffic just behind which may be trying to overtake you
  - traffic just in front of any vehicles you are planning to overtake
  - traffic coming towards you
- Overtake only when you can do so
  - safely
  - without causing other vehicles to slow down or alter course

✗ Faults you must avoid

You must not overtake when

- Your view of the road ahead is not clear
- You would have to exceed the speed limit

What the test requires

You must be able to meet and deal with oncoming traffic safely and confidently.

This mainly applies

- On narrow roads, or
- Where there are parked cars or other obstructions
- If there is an obstruction on your side of the road, or not enough room for two vehicles to pass safely
  - use the MSM routine
  - slow down and be prepared to stop
- When you need to stop, keep well back from the obstruction to give yourself
  - a better view of the road ahead
  - room to move off easily when the way is clear
- If possible when you are passing parked cars, allow at least the width of a car door

How the examiner will test you

For this aspect of driving, there is no special exercise.

The examiner will watch carefully and take account of your

- Use of the MSM routine
- Reactions to road and traffic conditions.
- Handling of the controls

Skills you must master

You must

- Show judgement when meeting oncoming traffic
- Be decisive when stopping and moving off
- Allow enough room when passing parked cars

Watch out for

- Doors opening
- Children running out
- Pedestrians stepping out
- Vehicles pulling out without warning

Wait here

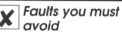 Faults you must avoid

Causing other vehicles to
- Slow down
- Swerve
- Stop

What the test requires

You must be able to cross the path of other vehicles safely and with confidence.

Crossing the path of other vehicles occurs mainly when you have to turn right into a side road or driveway.

You should

- Use the MSM routine
- Position your car correctly. Adjust your speed
- Keep as close to the centre of the road as is safe
- Watch out for approaching traffic. Stop if necessary.
- Watch out for pedestrians
  - crossing at the side road
  - on the pavement, if you are entering a driveway

 How the examiner will test you

For this aspect of driving, there is no special exercise.

The examiner will watch carefully and take account of your judgement of oncoming traffic.

Skills you must master

You must

- Show sound judgement when meeting oncoming traffic
- Be decisive when stopping and moving across

Faults you must avoid

- Causing other vehicles to
  - slow down
  - swerve
  - stop
- Cutting the corner

And you should not

- Go beyond the correct turning point before you begin to turn

What the test requires

You must

- Show courtesy and consideration towards pedestrians

At pelican crossings

You must

- Stop if the lights are red
- Give way to pedestrians crossing if the amber lights are flashing

At zebra crossings

You must

- Slow down and stop if there is anyone on the crossing

You should also

- Slow down and stop if anyone is waiting to cross
- Know the correct arm signal to use when slowing down

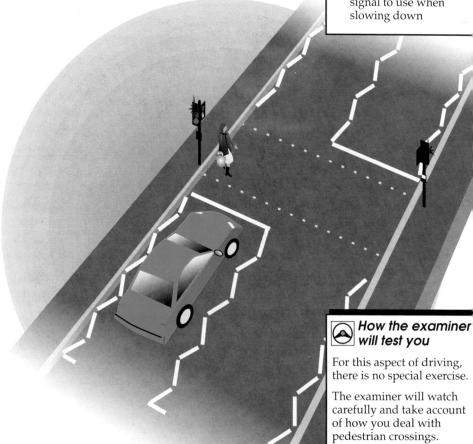

How the examiner will test you

For this aspect of driving, there is no special exercise.

The examiner will watch carefully and take account of how you deal with pedestrian crossings.

✔ Skills you must master

You must be able to

- Approach a pedestrian crossing at a controlled speed
- Stop safely when necessary
- Move off when it's safe, keeping a good lookout

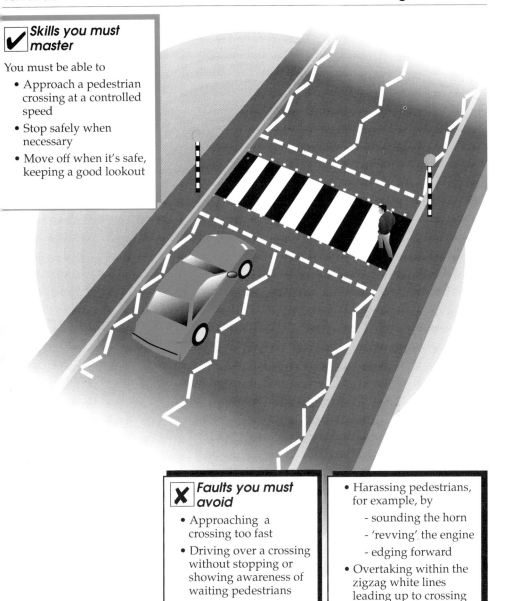

✗ Faults you must avoid

- Approaching a crossing too fast
- Driving over a crossing without stopping or showing awareness of waiting pedestrians
- Driving on to or blocking a crossing

- Harassing pedestrians, for example, by
  - sounding the horn
  - 'revving' the engine
  - edging forward
- Overtaking within the zigzag white lines leading up to crossing
- Waving at pedestrians to cross

Selecting a safe place to stop

 What the test requires

When you make a normal stop, you must be able to

- Select a place where you will not
  - obstruct the road
  - create a hazard
- Stop close to the edge of the road

 How the examiner will test you

For this aspect of driving, there is no special exercise.

The examiner will watch your driving and take account of your

- Use of the MSM routine
- Judgement in selecting a safe place to stop

 Skills you must master

You must know

- How and where to stop without causing inconvenience or danger to other road users

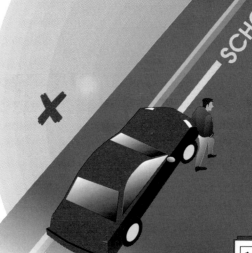

 Faults you must avoid

- Stopping with insufficient warning to other road users
- Causing danger or inconvenience to other road users when you stop

What the test requires

■ Awareness

You must
- Be aware of other road users at all times

■ Anticipation

You should try always to think ahead and plan ahead, and to
- Judge what other road users are going to do
- Predict how their actions would affect you
- React safely and in good time

 What the examiner wants to see

You must show
- Awareness of and consideration for all road users, and
- Anticipation of possible danger and concern for safety

For example

■ Pedestrians
- Give way to pedestrians when turning from one road into another
- Take particular care with the very young, the disabled, and the elderly. They may not have seen you and could step out

■ Cyclists
- When crossing bus or cycle lanes, take special care
- Take special care with children cycling

■ Motorcyclists
- Look out for motorcycles
  - in slow-moving traffic
  - coming up on your left
  - at junctions

■ Animals
- Take special care with people in charge of animals, especially horse riders

☒ Faults you must avoid
- Reacting late to road or traffic conditions rather than anticipating them
- Showing irritation with other road users, particularly cyclists or pedestrians
- Sounding your horn aggressively
- 'Revving' your engine or edging forward when waiting for pedestrians to cross

Section 3
The motorcycle test — preparation and training

Your provisional licence

Warning

If you want to learn to ride a motorcycle, make sure your provisional licence carries specific motorcycle entitlement.

If you obtained your provisional licence on or after 1st December, 1990, you are not allowed to

- Ride on the road, or
- Take your test

until you have attended a training course and reached a satisfactory standard.

Learning to ride — compulsory basic training

Compulsory basic training is for

- All learner motorcyclists, including those who wish to ride motorcycles with sidecars
- All learner moped riders

Approved Training Bodies

You must attend a course given by an Approved Training Body. These have

- Instructors who have passed the Driving Standards Agency course
- Sites approved by the Driving Standards Agency for off-road training

The Certificate of Completion

To gain a Certificate of Completion, you must

- Reach a satisfactory standard in each of five elements (see pages 37-41)
- Complete these in sequence, finishing with an on-road section

Your instructor will not allow you to progress to the next element until you are ready to do so.

Local courses and training organisations

Ask about local courses at

- Your local council (Road Safety Officer)
- Your motorcycle dealer

A free information pack is available from 'Bikeline' (Freefone 0800-400 483)

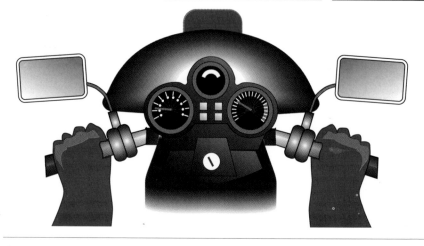

Element 1: Introduction

Before you do any practical training you must be told and understand

- The aims of the compulsory basic training course
- The importance of the right equipment and clothing
- The need to be clearly visible to other road users
- Legal requirements when riding on the road
- Why motorcyclists are more vulnerable than other road users
- The need to drive at correct speeds, according to road and traffic conditions
- The importance of reading and understanding the Highway Code

Your eyesight

You must be able to read in good daylight a number-plate

- Containing letters and figures 79.4 mm (3.1 inches) high
- At a distance of 20.5 metres (67 feet)
- With the aid of glasses or contact lenses if you normally wear them

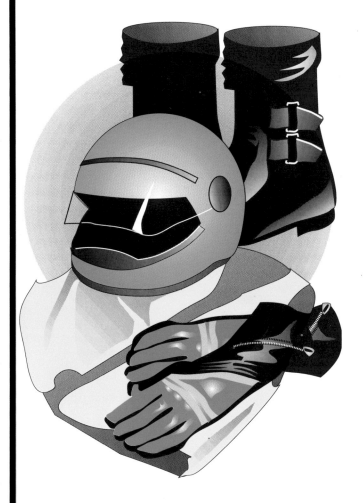

Compulsory training for motorcycle learners

 Element 2: Practical on-site training

You must become familiar with the motorcycle, its controls and how it works, and be able to

- Carry out basic machine checks, and be able to take the bike on and off the stand

- Wheel your motorcycle around to the left and right showing proper balance, and stop the motorcycle by braking

- Stop and start the engine satisfactorily

Element 3: Practical on-site riding

You must be able to

- Ride your motorcycle under control in a straight line, and bring it to a controlled stop
- Carry out controlled braking using both brakes
- Change gear satisfactorily
- Carry out rear observation correctly

- Carry out simulated left and right turns correctly using the routines
  - Observation-Signal-Manoeuvre (OSM)
  - Position-Speed-Look (PSL)
- Ride your motorcycle in a figure of eight circuit
- Ride your motorcycle slowly under control
- Bring your motorcycle to a stop under full control in an emergency

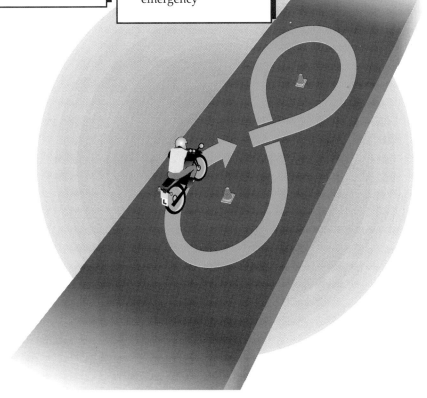

Compulsory training for motorcycle learners

**Element 4:
Practical on-road
training**

You must understand the
need to, and be able to

- Ride defensively and
  anticipate the actions of
  other road users

- Use rear observation at
  appropriate times

- Assume the correct
  road position when
  riding

- Leave sufficient space
  when following
  another vehicle

- Pay due regard to the
  effect of varying
  weather when riding

- Be aware of the various
  types of road surfaces
  you can meet

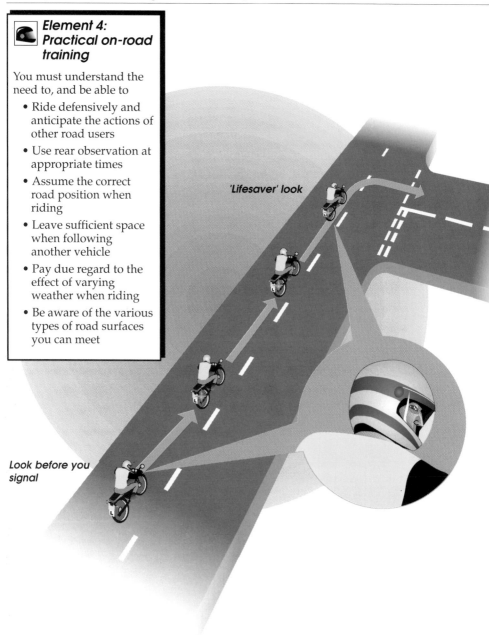

'Lifesaver' look

Look before you
signal

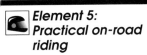

Element 5: Practical on-road riding

You must be able to ride safely under a variety of road and traffic conditions including as many of these as possible

- Roundabouts
- Junctions
- Pedestrian crossings
- Traffic lights
- Gradients
- Bends and obstructions

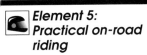

DRIVING STANDARDS AGENCY

Road Traffic Act 1988

| 000000 |

Certificate of Completion of an Approved Training Course for Motor Vehicles in Categories A and P

Driver Number of Candidate

Date and time of course completion   Hrs   Mins

Current name

Current address

                                                    Postcode

has successfully completed an approved training course for motor vehicles in categories A and P, prescribed for the purpose of Section 97 of the Road Traffic Act 1988 as amended by Section 6 of the Road Traffic (Driver Licensing and Information Systems) Act 1989.

Signature of Instructor   appointed to conduct such training

Initials and Surname (BLOCK CAPITALS)   No.

The successful candidate should sign in ink below in the presence of the instructor.

Signature

Official Stamp of Training Body   Site at which Course conducted and Site No.

Please read the notes overleaf   DL 196

An Executive Agency of the Department of Transport

The Certificate of Completion

When you complete this element you will be given a Certificate of Completion of an Approved Training Course.

You must either

- Send this with your application form when applying for the motorcycle test, or
- Present it when you attend for your test

Note: Your test will be cancelled if you don't.

The Approved Training Body will also wish to talk to you about the need for further training to prepare you for your test.

The motorcycle test

Special features

The driving test also applies to motorcycles. You should study Section 1 and the parts of Section 2 which apply to the motorcycle test.

The following are some extra requirements

Braking

You must be able combine the use of front and rear brakes correctly, in all weather conditions.

Make sure your instructor explains fully and you understand the correct braking techniques and their use.

Emergency Stop

- Apply the front brake just before the rear
- Apply both brakes effectively
- Stop the machine as quickly as possible without locking either wheel

U-Turn

After the emergency stop exercise the examiner will ask you to ride in a U-turn and stop on the other side of the road.

Slow Ride

You may be asked to ride as in slow-moving traffic for a short distance, if the examiner has not already seen you doing this in normal traffic.

Rear Observation

Even if you have mirrors fitted to your motorcycle, look over the appropriate shoulder to check the position of traffic before you

- Signal
- Change direction
- Slow down or stop

Take note of what you see and act on it.

Just looking is not enough!

How the examiner will test you

When you are taking the test, the examiner will follow you either on a motorcycle or in a car, except during the emergency stop exercise.

Your test will be carried out over a route covering a wide variety of traffic conditions.

Before the test you will be fitted with

- Earphones under your helmet
- A radio receiver on a waist belt

Driving is a life skill, and it will take you many years to gain full mastery of the skills set out here.

This syllabus lists the skills in which you must achieve basic competence in order to pass the Driving Test.

You must also have
- a thorough knowledge of the Highway Code and the motoring laws
- a thorough understanding of your responsibilities as a driver

This means that you must have real concern, not just for your own safety, but for the safety of all road users, including pedestrians.

If you learn with an Approved Driving Instructor (ADI), make sure he or she covers this syllabus fully.

1. Legal requirements

To learn to drive you must

i. be at least 17 years old. If you receive a monthly allowance for a disability you may start driving a car at 16.

ii. be able to read in good daylight, with glasses or contact lenses if you wear them, a motor vehicle number-plate
- 20.5m away
- with letters 79.4mm (3.1 inches) high

iii. be medically fit to drive

iv. hold a provisional licence or comply with the conditions for holding a provisional licence (see leaflet D100*)

v. ensure that the vehicle being driven
- is legally roadworthy
- has a current test certificate, if over the prescribed age
- is properly licensed with correct disc displayed

vi. make sure that the vehicle being driven is properly insured for its use

vii. display L plates which are visible from the front and the back of the vehicle

viii. be accompanied by a supervisor who
- has held a full UK licence for at least 3 years for the kind of vehicle being used
- is at least 21 years old

ix. wear a seat belt, unless granted an exemption, and see that all the seat belts in the vehicle and their anchorages and fittings are free from obvious defects

x. ensure that children under 14 are suitably restrained by an approved child restraint or an adult seat belt

xi. be aware of the legal requirement to notify medical conditions which could affect safe driving. If a vehicle has been adapted for disability, ensure that the adaptations are suitable to control the vehicle safely.

xii. know the rules on the issue, presentation or display of
- driving licences
- insurance certificates
- road excise licences

2. Car controls, equipment and components

You must

i. understand the function of the
- accelerator
- clutch
- gears
- footbrake
- handbrake
- steering

and be able to use these competently

ii. know the function of other controls and switches in the car that have a bearing on road safety and use them competently

iii. understand the meaning of the gauges and other displays on the instrument panel

iv. know the legal requirements for the vehicle

v. be able to carry out routine safety checks that do not require tools, and identify defects especially with
- steering
- brakes
- tyres
- seat belts
- lights
- reflectors
- direction indicators
- windscreen wipers and washers
- horn
- rear view mirrors
- speedometer
- exhaust system

vi. know the safety factors relating to vehicle loading

3. Road user behaviour

You must

i. know the most common causes of accidents

ii. know which road users are most at risk and how to reduce that risk

iii. know the rules, risks and effects of drinking and driving

iv. know the effect of fatigue, illness and drugs on driving performance

v. be aware of age dependent problems among other road users especially among children, teenagers and the elderly

---

*Leaflet D100 contains general information on driver licensing, and is free from DLVC Swansea or any Post Office.

Recommended syllabus for learning to drive

vi. be alert and be able to anticipate the likely actions of other road users and be able to suggest appropriate precautions

vii. be aware that courtesy and consideration towards road users are essential for safe driving

4. Vehicle characteristics

You must

i. know the most important principles concerning braking distances and road holding under various road and weather conditions

ii. know the handling characteristics of other vehicles with regard to stability, speed, braking and manoeuvrability

iii. know that some vehicles are less easily seen than others

iv. be able to assess the risks caused by the characteristics of other vehicles and suggest precautions that can be taken, for example

- large commercial vehicles pulling to the right before turning left
- blind spots for drivers of some commercial vehicles
- bicycles and motorcycles being buffeted by strong wind

5. Road and weather conditions

You must

i. know the particular hazards of driving
- in both daylight and dark
- on different types of road, for example
  - on single carriageway, including country lanes
  - on three-lane roads
  - on dual-carriageways and motorways

ii. gain experience in driving in urban and higher speed roads (but not motorways) in both daylight and darkness

iii. know which road surfaces provide the better or poorer grip when braking

iv. know the hazards caused by bad weather, for example
- rain
- fog
- snow
- icy roads
- strong cross winds

v. be able to assess the risks caused by road and traffic conditions, be aware of how the conditions may cause others to drive unsafely, and be able to take appropriate precautions

6. Traffic signs, rules and regulations

You must

i. have a sound knowledge of the meaning of traffic signs and road markings

ii. have a sound grasp of the traffic signs, for example
- speed limits
- parking restrictions
- zebra and pelican crossings

7. Car control and road procedure

You must have the knowledge and skill to carry out the following tasks
- in both daylight and darkness
- safely and competently
- making proper use of mirrors, observation, and signals

i. take necessary precautions before getting into or out of the vehicle

ii. before starting the engine
- carry out the 'cockpit drill' including fastening the seat belts
- take proper precautions

iii. start the engine and move off
- straight ahead and at an angle
- on the level and on uphill and downhill gradients

iv. select the correct road position for normal driving

v. take proper observation in all traffic conditions

vi. drive at a speed suitable for road and traffic conditions

vii. react promptly to all risks

viii. change traffic lanes

ix. pass stationary vehicles

x. meet, overtake and cross the path of other vehicles

xi. turn right and left, and at junctions, including crossroads and roundabouts

xii. drive ahead at crossroads and roundabouts

xiii. keep a safe separation gap when following other vehicles

xiv. act correctly at pedestrian crossings

xv. show proper regard for the safety of other road users, with particular care towards the most vulnerable

xvi. drive on both urban and rural roads and, where possible, dual carriageways — keeping up with the traffic flow where it is safe and proper to do so

xvii. comply with traffic regulations and traffic signs and signals given by the police, traffic wardens and other road users

xviii. stop the vehicle safely, normally and in an emergency, without locking the wheels

xix. turn the vehicle in the road to face the opposite way using the forward and reverse gears

xx. reverse the vehicle into a side turning keeping reasonably close to the kerb

xxi. park parallel to the kerb while driving in reverse gear

xxii. park the vehicle in a multistorey car park, or other parking bay, on the level, uphill and downhill, both in forward and reverse direction

xxiii. cross all types of railway level crossings

8. Additional knowledge

You must know

i. the importance of correct tyre pressures

ii. the action to avoid and correct skids

iii. how to drive through floods and flooded areas

iv. what to do if involved in an accident or breakdown including the special arrangements for accident and breakdown on motorways

v. basic first aid for use on the road as set out in the Highway Code

vi. the action to take to deter car thieves

9. Motorway driving

You must gain a sound knowledge of the special rules, regulations and driving techniques for motorway driving before taking your driving test.

After passing your test you should take motorway lessons with an ADI before driving unsupervised on motorways.

10. Points for riders of motorcycles and mopeds

You must master everything in sections 1 to 9, except the items which clearly do not refer to you.

In addition a learner rider must

i. know the safety factors relating to safety helmets and how to adjust the helmet correctly

ii. know the safety factors in wearing suitable clothing and in using goggles or a visor

iii. know the importance of rear observation
- by use of mirrors
- by looking over the shoulder
- including the life-saver look

iv. know how to lean while turning

v. be able to carry out additional safety checks for two-wheel vehicles, for example
- chain tension and condition
- condition of control cables
- steering-head play
- suspension
- wheels, and tightness of all nuts and bolts

vi. be able to use the front and rear brakes correctly

vii. be able to keep the machine balanced at all speeds

viii. be able to make a U-turn safely

ix. be able to wheel the machine, without the aid of the engine, by walking alongside it

x. be able to park and remove the machine from its stand

Section 5
Additional information

The condition of your vehicle

Your vehicle must be mechanically sound.

All equipment required by law must be fitted and working correctly. The engine must not be altered to run especially fast. This can cause loss of control.

The controls, seating or any equipment or articles in the car must be arranged so they do not interfere with the conduct of the test.

Your examiner must be able to see clearly through the rear window.

Seat belts

If the law requires your vehicle to have seat belts, make sure that

- They work properly

- They are in a clean and satisfactory condition

Wear your seat belt, unless you have a medical exemption certificate.

Reversing

You are allowed to remove your seat belt when reversing your vehicle. Make sure you fasten it immediately afterwards.

Examiner's seat belt

Your examiner will normally want to wear a seat belt, although examiners are exempt in some circumstances.

If your examiner is not able to fasten a seat belt, your test will be cancelled and you will lose your fee.

Left-hand drive vehicles

If you are driving a left-hand drive vehicle, take special care and make full use of your mirrors.

Commercial vehicles not suitable for a driving test

- Vehicles with only a driver's seat

- Loaded or partly loaded vehicles

- Vehicles over 7.5 tonnes in weight

Heavy goods and public service vehicles

If you want to drive

- A Heavy Goods Vehicle (HGV) over 7.5 tonnes permissible maximum weight, or

- A Public Service Vehicle (PSV),

read the leaflets on driving tests for these vehicles (DLG68 for HGV tests, and DLP 68 for PSV tests) available free from Driving Standards Agency Regional Offices.

Note

On 1st April, 1991, new regulations on HGV and PSV driving tests will come into force. Ask for details at your DSA Regional Office.

Motorcyclists

You must wear a safety helmet at all times when riding, unless you are a member of Sikh religion and wear a turban.

If your helmet has a visor, it must conform to the required BSI standard.

Test not conducted

You will lose your fee if you or your vehicle is responsible for the test not taking place

Bribery

It is a criminal offence to attempt to bribe an examiner in any way.

Additional information

If you pass

If you pass you will have shown your examiner that you can drive safely.

You must continue driving in the way you have been taught. With more experience you will certainly improve your driving skills.

Keep the right attitude towards other road users.

Once you have sufficient experience and training you should aim to pass an advanced driving test and develop the standard to make it a life skill. For further information on Advanced Driving contact the Institute of Advanced Motoring (IAM) or ROSPA.

Ask your driving instructor for lessons in motorway driving. This is important, because you must get experience in driving on motorways.

If you fail

Your driving will not have been up to the standard required.

You will have made mistakes which could have caused danger on the road.

Your examiner will

- Give you a Statement of Failure which lists these mistakes

- Tell you briefly why they are listed, but cannot discuss them in any detail

Study the Statement and look up the sections in this book. Show the statement to your ADI, who will help you to correct the faults.

Your ADI will not concentrate on the faults, but will aim to continue to improve all aspects of your driving before you retake the test.

Listen to your ADI's advice, and get as much practice as you can.

You must wait one calendar month before you can be tested on a vehicle of the same category.

Section 6
List of DSA offices and other useful addresses

DSA Head Office
Stanley House
Talbot Street
Nottingham
NG1 5GU
Tel: 0602-474222
Fax: 0602-485734

DSA Regional Offices
Scotland
83 Princes Street
Edinburgh
EH2 2ER
Tel: 031-225-5418
Fax: 031-225-5494 Ext 312

**North Eastern Region
(Newcastle)**
Westgate House
Westgate Road
Newcastle-upon-tyne
NE1 1TW
Tel: 091-261-0031
Fax: 091-222-0824

North Eastern Region (Leeds)
Hillcrest House
386 Harehills Lane
Leeds
LS9 6NF
Tel: 0532-499433
Fax: 0532-489607

North Western Region
Portcullis House
Seymour Grove
Stretford
Manchester
M16 0NE
Tel: 061-872-2333
Fax: 061-872-0910 Ext 435

West Midlands Region
Cumberland House
200 Broad Street
Birmingham
B15 1TD
Tel: 021-631-2020
Fax: 021-631-3300 Ext 415

Eastern Region (Nottingham)
Birkbeck House
14-16 Trinity Square
Nottingham
NG1 4BA
Tel: 0602-475511
Fax: 0602-475511 Ext 220

Eastern Region (Cambridge)
Terrington House
13-15 Hills Road
Cambridge
CB2 1NP
Tel: 0223-321396
Fax: 0223-358922 Ext 228

South Wales
Caradog House
1-6 St Andrews Place
Cardiff
Glamorgan
CF1 3PW
Tel: 0222-225186
Fax: 0222-371675

Western Region
The Gaunts House
Denmark Street
Bristol
BS1 5DR
Tel: 0272-221066
Fax: 0272-297221 Ext 418

South Eastern Region
Ivy House
3 Ivy Terrace
Eastbourne
BN21 4QT
Tel: 0323-21471
Fax: 0323-21057

Metropolitan Region
PO Box 643
Charles House
375 Kensington High Street
London
W14 8QU
Tel: 071-835-1474
Fax: 071-605-0499

Other useful addresses
**Approved Driving Instructors
National Joint Council**
The Secretary
41, Edinburgh Road
Cambridge CB4 1QR
Tel: 0223-359079

**Driving Instructors
Association**
The Secretary
Safety House
Beddington Farm Road
Croydon
CRO 4XZ
Tel: 081-665-5151

Institute of Advanced Motorists
IAM House
359, Chiswick High Road
London
W4 4HS
Tel: 081-994-4403

Motor Schools Association of Great Britain Ltd
General Manager
182A Heaton Moor Road
Stockport
Cheshire
SK4 4DU
Tel: 061-443-1611

National Association of Approved Driving Instructors
Willow Garth
Sutton Lane
Barmby Moor
York
YO4 5HX
Tel: 07595-8194

Royal Automobile Club
Registrar of Instructors
The Manager
PO Box 100
RAC House
South Croydon
CR2 6XW
Tel: 081-686-2525

The Royal Society for the Prevention of Accidents (ROSPA)
The Priory
Queensway
Birmingham
B4 6BS
Tel: 021-200-2461

Printed in the United
Kingdom by H.M.S.O.
Dd 293172 c2500 11-9C

Your Driving Test